Printed in the United States

ISBN 978-1-105-62361-5

Cover Photograph by Paul Garza

Cover Design by Jennifer Garza

Interior design by Paul Garza

Text and organization by Jennifer Garza

Edited by Paul Garza

Typography: times roman

20% of the profit of this book will benefit the Lodi Food Bank

Visit us on the Web at www.everythingwomenknow.com

Everything Women know about Men

Incredible new findings after years of research!

By Dr. Paul Garza

To my family and wonderful wife who inspired me to write this book

Thanks for putting up with me!

This book is intentionally blank.

Pa

Pa

Pag

Printed in the United States

ISBN 978-1-105-62361-5

Cover Photograph by Paul Garza

Cover Design by Jennifer Garza

Interior design by Paul Garza

Text and organization by Jennifer Garza

Edited by Paul Garza

Typography: times roman

20% of the profit of this book will benefit the Lodi Food Bank

Visit us on the Web at www.everythingwomenknow.com

Everything Women know about Men

Incredible new findings after years of research!

By Dr. Paul Garza

To my family and wonderful wife who inspired me to write this book

Thanks for putting up with me!

This book is intentionally blank.

Pa

Pa

Pa

www.ingramcontent.com/pod-product-compliance
Ingram Content Group UK Ltd.
Pitfield, Milton Keynes, MK11 3LW, UK
UKHW041917190726
13854UKWH00003B/1300